"Every place on earth bespeaks its own rhythm of life.

Every locality has its own spirit. There is no accounting for the mysterious magnetism that

draws and holds us to that one locality we know as our heart's home."

—Frank Waters, Mountain Mystery

Open Space at Davidson Ditch and Cherryvale Road

Boulder's Geologic Heritage

THE PROCESS STARTED more than 1.75 billion years ago. Through the ages, the conflicting geologic forces of uplift and erosion have worked against each other to shape the landscape that we exist upon today. Mountains larger than the Rockies rose, bent, folded, and then were either worn flat or curved into gentle rolling hills. Volcanoes spewed lava and ash, and eventually, disappeared. Dunes and beaches were formed as seas encroached from the east and then receded. Worked by the sea over centuries, the dunes and beaches became brittle sandstone. As time passed, the dinosaurs roamed the land and then vanished. Somewhere between sixty and ninety million years ago layers of sedimentary rock tipped at a 50° angle, creating the Fountain Formation (the Flatirons) and the Dakota Formation (Echo Rocks) along a fault line running north and south. According to John and Halka Chronic, who wrote *The Geologic Story of the NCAR Site*, "The uplift in Colorado did not come quickly by human standards, although it may have taken only a few million years." Streams formed by rain and snow melt from glaciers carved deep v-shaped canyons where South Boulder, Bear, and Boulder Creeks run today. Alluvial fans of glacial debris formed terraces and outwashed plains to the east of Boulder. In its most recent form this is the landscape the city sits on today.

The Flatirons through Royal Arch

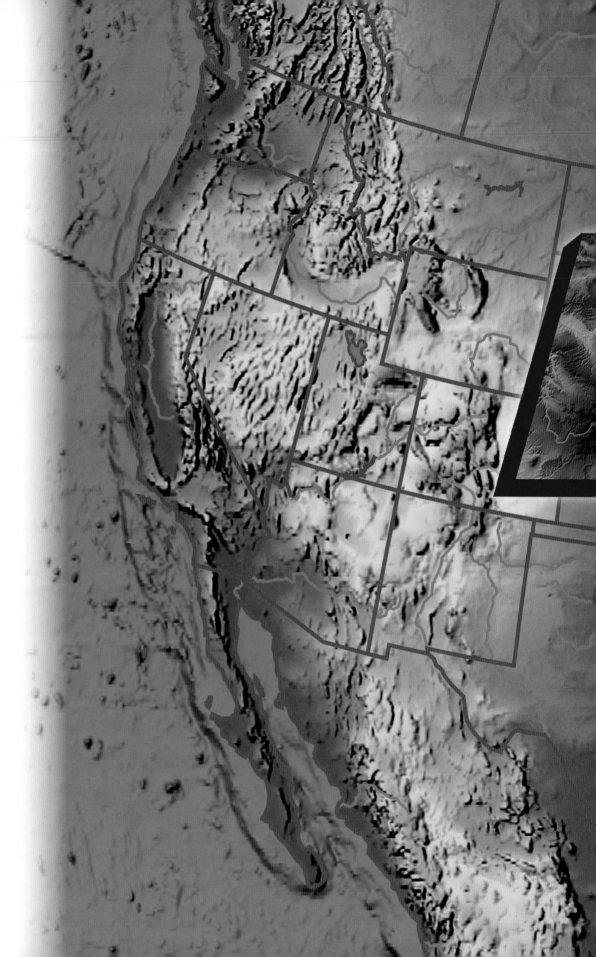

Destination Boulder

Boulder is located near the heart of Colorado, in the western half of the United States. This city can be found 33 miles north of Denver, the state's capital, and a 45 minute drive from Denver International Airport. Nestled at the base of the Rocky Mountains, Boulder is 20 miles due east of the Continental Divide, 39 miles from Rocky Mountain National Park, and lies on the western edge of the Great Plains. Boulder is home to 96,000 inhabitants, boasts 7,000 acres of mountain parks, and is surrounded by 27,000 acres of Open Space preserves, with no adjoining town touching its city limits. Located at 105°15' west longitude and 40° north latitude, the city is 1,250 miles from San Francisco, California; 1,850 miles from New York City; 675 miles from Mexico; and 850 miles from Canada. Its closest neighboring cities are Broomfield, Lafayette, Longmont, Louisville, Nederland, Niwot, and Superior. Boulder's sister cities include: Yamagata, Japan; Jalapa, Nicaragua; Lhasa, Tibet; and Dushanbe, Tajikistan.

Boulder

Colorado

Kid's Fishing Pond, Boulder Creek

BOULDER

HEART & SOUL
PEOPLE & PLACE

Story & Photography by
Robert Castellino

Forward by
Josie Heath & Will Toor

Boulder skyline, Valmont Dyke

Whispering River, LLC
Boulder, Colorado
Phone (303) 440-7711
Fax (303) 440-3431

Robert Castellino, *Publisher*

Designed by Dave Dombrowski & Elizabeth O. Taylor
Edited by Tambra Nelson & Polly Christensen
Illustration and watercolor by Charmayne Bernhardt

Printed in Hong Kong
through Bolton Associates, San Rafael, California

ISBN 1-879914-96-4 (Paperback)
ISBN 1-879914-95-6 (Hardcover)

Library of Congress Card Catalog Number: 98-090186

First Printing, 1998

Dedication

This book is dedicated to all those who have shaped the heart and soul of Boulder through their vision, desire, and dedication to maintain its natural beauty and way of life that makes it our home.

For my Son, Joren

Dakota Ridge

TABLE OF CONTENTS

Rainbow over Boulder, Flagstaff Road

INTRODUCTION
A VIEW FROM TWO PERSPECTIVES

Josie Heath and Will Toor have written the introduction to Boulder—Heart & Soul—People & Place. *Each offers a unique perspective about Boulder and what it means to have made this place home. The sense of place they found is undeniable. Is it any different than the way you found Boulder? Is it possible once you visited Boulder you are destined to return and make this your home? Undoubtedly, there is a deep-rooted sense that links us all to this place, regardless of our origins or the reasons we came. May their words join you to the story and photographs gracing these pages.*

Will Toor, *Deputy Mayor*
Boulder, Colorado, 1998

I can still remember my first glimpse of Boulder as I rode over the hill on US 36 in the summer of 1980. My intention wasn't to stay, but the car I was hitching a ride in broke down on 28th and Colorado. I decided to spend a few days, and that was going to be it. Seventeen years later, I'm still here. One of the first things that impressed itself upon me about this city was its spectacular physical beauty.

Many people have similar stories—they came to Boulder by accident, and found that it somehow became home. The same could be said of many towns in the west—places where the air is clean, where open lands surround the towns, and the pace is a little slower. What makes Boulder different is that forty years ago the people who lived here started pulling together to preserve some of these features. At a time when most towns in the west were run by the boosters (those who followed in Gilpin's footsteps) our citizens began to create a vision of a town where community and the public good were as important as commerce.

In the 1950s, citizens pushed for the "blue line," an imaginary line running through the foothills just west of town. Beyond this boundary, no city services would be supplied. A few years later, in one of our true defining moments, citizens created Boulder's Open Space Program. The people voted to tax themselves for the purpose of purchasing open lands on the outskirts of the city, to preserve them for future generations. Only after three decades of rapid growth, other communities along the Front Range are beginning to preserve their open space.

Over the years many political shifts have taken place, but love for our open space and mountain parks has been a bedrock value. We have voted several times to tax ourselves more, to use our collective buying power to preserve our surroundings. We may bicker with each other about how to manage the land, and certainly many areas are harmed by too many visitors—but at least the land is still here.

This preservation of land, more than any other act we have taken, has kept this an area of beauty and life. Imagine what Boulder would be like if houses spilled across the plains from here to our neighboring cities. Look up at the foothills to the West on a summer night and imagine a sea of lights instead of the quiet dark. Make no mistake—what we have is not an accident. It took a conscious act of will by a people determined to create a town worthy of the landscape.

Josie Heath

Boulder, Colorado, 1998

In the following pages, you will read and sense the beauties of Boulder. Words and pictures alone, however, cannot capture the spirit of Boulder, the spirit that binds us together into a community. That spirit comes from each of us and flows back into the community and helps define who we are.

What is it about a sense of place? People are shaped inevitably by the place they call home: maybe they listen for the Lexington Avenue subway in their sleep; perhaps they call on the meditation of ocean surf coming and going on the beach; maybe they need the big sky of the plains to know where they are. In Boulder, it's the presence of nature, of mountains and plains meeting, of the seasons interrupting one another.

We each have places here that we treasure. For some, it is a place to glimpse the powdery snow on the Flatirons, to hear squeals of joy from children on sleds. For others, it might be hiking a favorite trail to see the early morning's coral glow of dawn on the Rockies, or sitting in a meadow of wildflowers, or climbing a granite rock wall. When we are in these spots, our spirits soar. Recharged, re-energized, we are ready for the challenges ahead. Does this magic fuel the entrepreneurial spirit so evident here? Our non-profit community is unusually creative, our public sector has many firsts for innovative "good government" projects, and our thriving private sector, the envy of many, is fueled by the ingenuity of creative folks who invent new ideas to support their staying here.

We in Boulder can give our children wonderful gifts—such as knowing they will remember walks on Open Space lands, and will know the names of flowers, trees, and rocks. We as a community can help set their standards for things like clean water, and help them to understand the sacrifices, work, and compromises that assure it. We hope, as all parents do, that these gifts will help our children return home again, and while they are away, help them to carry a sense of wonder and awe in natural settings everywhere. Our greatest legacy here would be if our children have that same commitment to preserving nature wherever they are.

These beautiful surroundings nourish our spirit. We plan for the future because we want to be involved with shaping our future. We want to preserve and protect this beautiful place for our children, grandchildren, and for generations to come. Robert Castellino's love for Boulder, his home, has given us all a great gift. He has captured Boulder's heart and soul, people and places, with the magic of his camera. Read and enjoy!

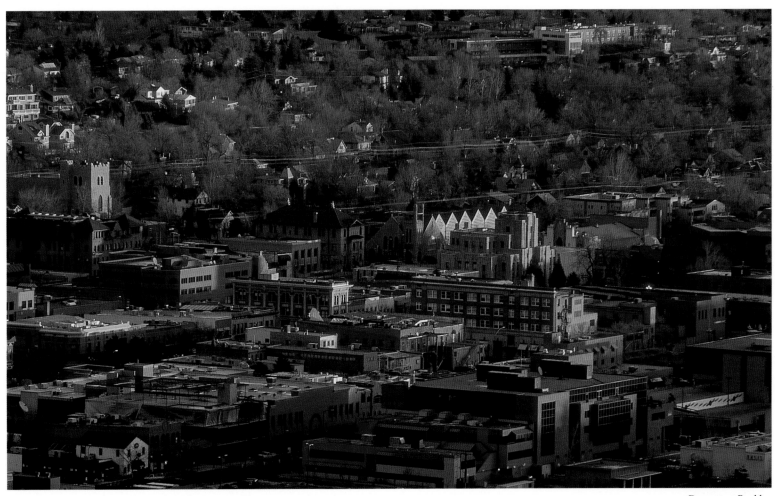

Downtown Boulder

Pearl Street circa 1890, photo courtesy Boulder Historical Society
Photograph by Joseph Bevier Sturtevant, "Rocky Mountain Joe"

BOULDER'S
BRIEF HISTORY

Imagine this place ...

I MAGINE YOURSELF RIDING a horse into the Boulder Valley on a warm spring afternoon three hundred years ago. You have just made your way over a ridge east of town where Arapahoe Road and 63rd Street intersect today. Since early in the morning you have seen the jagged, red rocks of the monolithic Flatirons thrusting skyward from the floor of the plains. Looming large on the distant horizon, the Continental Divide lies beyond the foothills still clad with a heavy mantle of winter snow. The valley and surrounding hills are carpeted with lush green grasses. Streams winding through the wetlands are swollen with spring run-off from the thaw high in the peaks. Large herds of buffalo, antelope, elk, and deer graze lazily across the buttes and valleys. The silence is broken as large flocks of geese and ducks fly out from the wetlands just below you. You are struck by the magnificent beauty of this place and the abundance of wildlife is almost beyond your comprehension.

Charmayne Thévenet Bernhardt

Native Americans' Devastating Decline

THE FIRST NOMADIC Native Americans, possibly from the Southern Arapaho or Cheyenne tribes, might have found the Boulder area this way while seeking escape from the harsh winters on the high plains. Most notable to the Boulder Valley is Chief Niwot (a.k.a. Chief Left Hand), a revered, legendary Southern Arapaho who lived here between the 1830s and early 1860s. He was raised in a nomadic tribe noted for their trading business with other plains natives and with Anglo-European mountain men and traders. Chief Niwot, an accomplished and confident man who learned to speak English and the languages of many plains tribes in his youth, was a skilled peacemaker. Extensive accounts of Chief Niwot and the devastating decline of his people are well documented in Margaret Coel's original book, *Chief Left Hand—Southern Arapho*. She placed him as a prominent figure at the center of controversy between the Native Americans, and "the hard single-minded" goldseekers of the Gold Rush on the high plains of Colorado. According to Coel, "Chief Niwot was one of the first of his people to acknowledge the inevitability of

Chief Niwot Sculpture
9th & Canyon, Sculpture Park

white man's presence on the plains, and thereafter to espouse a policy of adamant peacefulness (if not, finally, friendship) toward the newcomers."

Chief Niwot moved his people from Beaver Creek on the northeastern Colorado plains and he set up camp along Boulder Creek in early November of 1858. Upon arriving, he learned of Captain Thomas Aikin's encampment near the mouth of Boulder Canyon, known today as Settlers' Park. According to Coel, "Left Hand possessed a strong sense of responsibility toward his people and worried greatly about their future. In a short time he gained a reputation among goldseekers as an intelligent, honest, and trustworthy man." Chief Left Hand found the "iron clad determination" of the goldseekers different from that of any Anglo-Europeans he had met before. Coel makes note that, more than most of the settlers who came before the goldseekers, these "Anglo-European newcomers" were neither equipped nor suited to take on the harsh environment they believed held the riches of their future fortune. Yet, in a few short years these settlers poured into the Denver and Boulder areas and further west (first by the tens, and

"The Indian saw in the westward march of civilization his rights diminishing; the settlements along the streams meant loss of water. He saw his hunting ground broken up and the game going west before the white man's advance. He is a reader of signs, and in these signs he read 'the beginning of the end.'"
—Julia S. Lambert

20

then, hundreds of thousands). Often devastating all that came before them, the white settlers destroyed large tracks of indigenous grasslands and slaughtered herds of buffalo, leaving carcasses strewn across the land. To make matters worse, the settlers brought diseases unknown to the native immune systems and countless numbers of natives died. Many Native Americans also may have perished at the hands of the U.S. Army Infantry and in skirmishes with goldseekers. Although adept at life on the western plains, and able to survive well within the ways of the natural world, the natives could not endure this combination of inhumane treatment and diseases.

This was a tenuous time for the settlers and natives alike. The settlers needed to maintain free and open trading routes for commerce to maintain a flow of life sustaining supplies. Native leaders struggled with their fatigued, embittered and battle-weary people to maintain peace among themselves and with the settlers. At this moment in history, the cry of the wild west died and the white man's world came crashing down on the natives. Ultimately, this was the turning point in the west for Chief Left Hand and his people when they were either moved to arid and inhospitable lands by the U.S. Federal Government or massacred at Sand Creek in November 1864. White settlers in resource abundant areas like Boulder replaced the Native Americans almost overnight.

Celebrative Native American Dance
Photo made in honor of all
Native American's presence in Boulder.

Chautauqua Park circa 1899, photo courtesy Boulder Historical Society
Photograph by Joseph Bevier Sturtevant, *"Rocky Mountain Joe"*

"People are shaped inevitably by the place they call home."
—Josie Heath

Sunset Hill circa 1895, photo courtesy Boulder Historical Society
Joseph Bevier Sturtevant, *"Rocky Mountain Joe"*

Contemporary Boulder Established

THE DATE WAS February 10, 1859 when the Boulder City Town Company was formed. Under its direction, the Boulder area became, for all intents and purposes, a trading post for goldseekers. Gold found at Central City, Gold Hill and Ward continued the rush for riches near Boulder. The once wide open, unspoiled landscape as it was known by the Southern Arapaho, Cheyenne, Pawnee, Ute, Kiowa and Comanche people was forever changed as gold mines appeared throughout mountain communities. The Boulder area was no longer a native wintering ground and a sacred place, but became home to newcomers whose vision of stewardship was quite different.

Mining proved to be difficult and exhausting work, so much that many goldseekers left the mines and returned to the valley to try their hand at agriculture, creating a new

larged boundaries. A mayor was elected, and the town's name was changed from Boulder City to Boulder. The University of Colorado Board of Trustees held its first meeting on January 29, 1870. By 1877 the first University structure—then called Old Main—was built, and the first group of students began classes. A mix of characters began meeting at the university to create the foundation for a community deeply concerned with economic growth, higher education, personal well being and the sustainability of the natural surroundings.

Between 1870 and 1900, Boulder grew in size from 360 to nearly 6,150 people. A group of Texas schoolteachers joined Boulder's leaders and railroad officials to found the Texas–Colorado Chautauqua in 1898 as a cultural retreat from the hot dry and dusty Texas summers. After Flagstaff Mountain, Chautauqua Park (originally named Texado

14th & Pearl Street circa 1922, photo courtesy Boulder Historical Society. Photography by Ed Tangen

pulse. The fertile soil, mild winter climate and reliable water supply flowing from the mountain streams made farming a sustainable way of living. The new settlement struggled through the 1860s due to inadequate facilities to mill the gold ore. During the 1870s Boulder emerged from its infancy as civic and private enterprise surged to the forefront. The town was incorporated on November 4, 1871, and then reincorporated in February 1878 with en-

Park) was Boulder's first public park and consisted of eighty acres of land. Here the Texans built an auditorium, living quarters and a dining hall, surrounded by the beautiful foothill property. The Chautauquans spent their summers studying literature and science, attending art shows and musical concerts and enjoying day-long hikes in the foothills and mountains. The spirit of Chautauqua flourished through the turn of the Twentieth Century and stood the test of time,

Broadway & Pearl Street circa 1921, photo courtesy Boulder Historical Society
Photograph by Ed Tangen

having celebrated its hundredth birthday in 1998. The development of Chautauqua Park promoted the expansion of Boulder open space and mountain parks. Soon Boulder became renown for its scenic beauty and ultimately its progressive position protecting the natural landscape as a part of its city growth plan.

The railroad pushed into Boulder and then westward to the mining towns. Two railroads reached the city in 1873—the Colorado Central Railroad and the Denver & Boulder Valley Railroad. As the automobile made its way out of the Industrial Age, some of these train routes gave way to roads. Although roads into Boulder were originally established as supply routes, locals and tourists eventually used them to escape into the high Colorado Rockies for recreation.

Except for the thousands of tourists visiting the Boulder area each year to enjoy its natural beauty, Boulder's popula-tion levels followed the boom and bust cycles of the regional and national economy. Each passing generation has faced challenges of how best to develop, maintain and sustain Boulder's exceptional resources. Fortunately, the past stewards who have managed the development of Boulder, have done so with great concern for its natural environment. Boulder is a beautiful place to live, work and play. A unique balance has been struck to maintain the city's pristine landscape and to restrict unbridled urban development. Since Boulder's inception, many people have made an indelible contribution in shaping this progressive city. Boulder is made up of the heart and soul of its people making it a place we love and share today.

Summer view from Sunset Hill
photo courtesy Boulder Historical Society

"Boulder gained its name due to the jumble of large boulders
in the lower part of the canyon."
—**Chamber of Commerce Guide, 1947**

*"Everybody needs beauty …
places to play in and pray in
where Nature may heal and
cheer and give strength
to the body and soul alike."*
—John Muir

The Flatirons

Spring

Summer

THE SEASONS

Fall

Winter

As THE SEASONS change so changes the composition of Boulder's character throughout the year. With the arrival of each season there is a new feeling and perspective to the everyday going here. The timeless adage, "wait ten minutes and the weather will change," is as true for Boulder as when it was originally coined for Colorado. The transitions between seasons are as dramatic and as distinct as the seasons themselves. Rare are the times when the movement from one to the next is subtle or drawn out. However, there are warm days hinting to us spring is on the way in the midst of winter, and fall has shortened summer before its time when temperatures drop unexpectedly. Sometimes the character summer appears more like the rainy wet tropics than the high alpine arid climate as we know it. Yet through them all life continues to flow pausing only momentarily to grab a short breath or a sigh before moving on. These are the signs of the seasons consistently changing Boulder through the continuum of time.

The beauty of each season is more than one could anticipate. The colors range from rich and vibrant to cool and fresh. Only once every so often during each season does gloom set in tempering the spirit. Each season calls out for us to play in the open spaces, mountain parks and city streets. Rare are the harsh days that stop us in our tracks from getting out and moving around. The snow falls, the flowers bloom, the grasses green, the rivers rush, the heat rises, the wind blows, and the leaves turn all in perfect sychronicity. Some to the pleasure of one and the discomfort of another. Yet certain as the weather changes there is one day each season that anyone would say is beautiful.

Away from the city, the subtle and intricate nature of the seasons are found in wild open spaces and mountain parks. There are a range of diverse bio-niches at different elevations from the plains through the foothills to the high alpine mountain peaks. Flowers bloom, trees bud, grasses green and leaves change at varying times throughout a single season. Spring appears to be happening in the midst of summer just 1,500 feet higher than the plains, and fall appears earlier in the higher climbs by up to a full month compared to the city itself. The change in seasons are more than marking the passing of time as we turn the pages of our calendars; subtlty, they change before our very eyes everyday all year.

Bronze Fountain on Pearl Street Mall

Poppy Garden, University Hill Neighborhood

Spring

Sunny Day, Pearl Street Mall

Iris Intimacy

"Only those who partake in the harmony within their souls know the harmony that runs through nature."

—Tao Te Ching

Sprinkler Shower—Chautauqua Park

Spring Tulips—Pearl Street

Prairie Primrose—Blue Lake

Summer

Flagstaff Mountain

Varsity Pond—University of Colorado

The Maiden—Eldorado Springs

Wild Poppies – Chautauqua Meadow

The Dining Hall—Chautauqua Park

"*What we see depends mainly on what we look for.*"
—John Lubbock

California Poppies, Mapleton Hill Garden

37

Autumn

Fall Foliage —Blue Baird Shelter

"Weave the golden cloth of dreams
with the silken threads of sweet memories."
—**Paramahansa Yogananda**

Fall Colors, Columbia Cemetery – 9th & College

Sunrise at Chautauqua Meadow

Fall Collage, Pearl Street Mall

Sunrise at the White Cliffs, East Boulder Creek

"A gentle and wise guide always shines the light on the most forgiving pathway home—even if it appears as ruthless compassion. Home is where the true sense of who you are resides. Know the core of your soul. Seek this place out with immense passion and never quit."

—Robert L. Castellino

Eldorado Springs

"The sun shines not

on us, but in us." –John Muir

Cityscape, Sunrise at Sunset Hill

Winter

"Of vital importance to creating change is the basic act of paying attention to who we are and how we interact with the world. We need to break free from our numbness and begin to let our sensitivity inform, rather than disable us."

—Dawn Griffin

North Shore Sunrise–Boulder Reservoir

Sunrise Continental Divide –Boulder Reservoir

"When despair for the world grows in me
and I wake in the night at the least sound
in fear of what my life and my children's lives may be,
I go and lie down where the wood drake
rests in his beauty on the water, and the great heron feeds.
I come into the peace of wild things
who do not tax their lives with forethought
of grief. I come into the presence of still water.
And I feel above me the day-blind stars
waiting with their light. For a time
I rest in the grace of the world, and am free."

—**Wendell Berry**

CU Rowing Team–Boulder Reservoir

Flatiron Sunrise–Boulder Reservoir

Snow Crystals and The Flatirons–Chautauqua Park

Sunrise–North Shore, Boulder Reservoir

"The best thing we have learned from nearly five hundred years of contact with the American wilderness is restraint, the willingness to hold our hand: to visit such places for our souls' good, but leave no tracks."

—**Wallace Stegner**

Sunrise–East Shore Boulder Reservoir

HEART & SOUL – PEOPLE & PLACE

Humans are tuned for relationship, the eyes, the skin, the tongue, ears and nostrils—all are gates where our body receives the nourishment of otherness. This landscape of shadowed voices, these feathered bodies and antlers and tumbling streams—these breathing shapes are our family, the beings with whom we are engaged, with whom we struggle and suffer and celebrate.

—Anonymous,
Boulder Creek Path–CU Research Center

Heart & Soul—People & Place

AT THE CENTER of Boulder's heart sits a core community of people committed to its well-being. This community includes people who make their homes here today and is strongly influenced by the past generations that have lived here since Boulder's inception 140 years ago. These past inhabitants include the nomadic Southern Arapaho and Cheyenne, the gold-seekers and the settlers moving westward. Boulder's pulse appears to emanate from its citizens' passion to create positive change through activism and participation that mutually benefits and affects the world around them.

The unique soul of Boulder thrives in the rugged and wide open western landscape. This dramatic environment shapes our character as a community as much as we have sculpted a city to blend within it. The Mountain Parks and Open Space departments managed by the City of Boulder maintain the natural beauty of the environment around us. Sustaining these magnificent treasures (our mountains, prairie grasslands, coniferous forests, the Flatirons (fountain formations), wild creatures, and clear running creeks are important daily reminders of the quality of life we enjoy. Natural places like these inspire a sense of awe, humbleness and reverence in all of us. They are our natural connection, grounding us to our western wilderness inheritance. Hopefully, this rich heritage will continue to be stewarded with concern for visitors and future generations that will make Boulder their home.

Pearl Street Mall

Shakespeare Festival, Norlin Quadrangle—University of Colorado

"*How dependent we are on each others' breath! I feel this vividly as I draw in slowly the air you have just breathed and every other creature has used to create one atmosphere.*"

–Anonymous,
Boulder Creek Path-The Connecting Point

Gregory Canyon Vista

Bridge at Children's Fishing Pond, Boulder Creek

Boulder Creek Bike & Pedestrian Path

Kinetics Conveyance Race, Boulder Reservoir

"*If you are seeking creative ideas, go out walking. Angels whisper to a man when he goes for a walk.*"

—Raymond Inmon

Mapleton Elementary

Fall Shadows on Pearl Street Mall

Too much time is spent in rushing, in getting no where.
Very few of us stop, think, and try to find out
what life can give us.

—Paramahansan Yogananda

Busker on Pearl Street Mall

Store Front—Pearl Street Mall

"We are creatures shaped by our experiences; we like what we know, more often than we know what we like."

—Wallace Stegner

Folsom Field—University of Colorado

"Twenty years from now you will be more disappointed by the things you didn't do than by the ones you did do. So throw off the bowlines. Sail away from the safe harbor. Catch the trade winds in your sails. Explore. Dream. Discover."

—Mark Twain

Scott Carpenter Park

Campus Roof Tops—Flatirons

Catching Snow Flakes—Chautauqua Park

"*If I had my child* to raise all over again, I'd fingerpaint more, and point the finger less. I'd do less correcting, and more connecting. I'd take my eyes off my watch, and watch with my eyes. I would care to know less, and know to care more. I'd take more hikes and fly more kites. I'd stop playing serious, and seriously play. I would run through more fields and gaze at more stars. I'd do more hugging, and less tugging. I would be firm less often, and affirm much more. I'd build self-esteem first, and the house later. I'd teach less about the love of power, and more about the power of love."

—Diane Loomans, *Full Esteem Ahead*
Courtesy Celestial Seasonings

Hikers on Arapahoe Peak

Embracing Winter—Blue Baird Shelter

Summer Concert—Chautauqua Auditorium

Afternoon Conversation—The Bridge at Varsity Pond , University of Colorado

The Holidays on Pearl Street Mall

*"What wisdom can you find
that is greater than Kindness?"*
**–Jean-Jacques Rousseau,
Courtesy Celestial Seasonings**

Dushanabe Tea House, 14th Street

Finish at the Bolder Boulder

Hiking at Sunrise—Dakota Formation, Settlers Park

Telemark Skiing at Chautauqua Park

Kayaking on Boulder Creek at Eben Fine Park

Summer Sunset—Baseline and 5th streets

Painting Poppies—McClintock Trail behind Chautauqua Auditorium

"In the first light of morning, may we
remember the magic.
May the white sun explode through
our eyes on the name of our love.
May we remember.
And in the evening, when darkness
settles into our bones, stars
kindling the beginnings of
dreams, may we remember.
May we always remember."

—**Stan Rushworth**

Family Walk—Sunrise at Chautauqua Park

4th of July—Folsom Field, University of Colorado

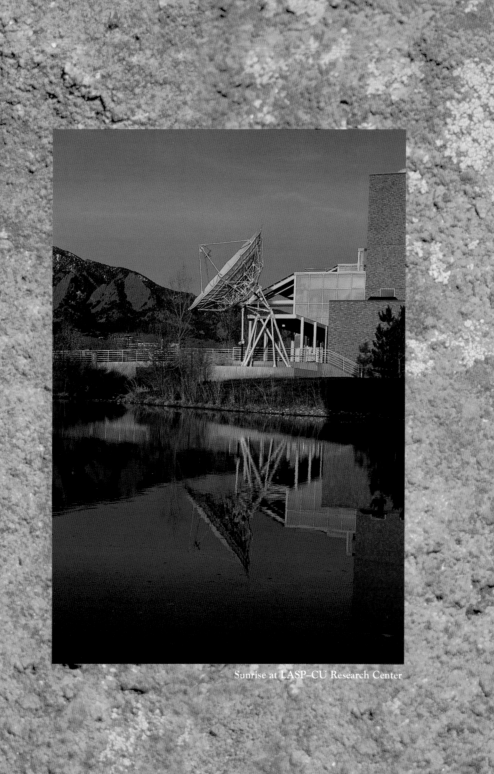

Sunrise at LASP–CU Research Center

ECOLOGY & COMMERCE

Sustainability is an economic state where the demands placed upon the environment by people and commerce can be met without reducing the capacity of the environment to provide for future generations.

—Paul Hawkins,
The Ecology of Commerce

ALONG WITH NATURE'S gift of beautiful surroundings, the city of Boulder is blessed with people who share an entrepreneurial spirit toward commerce. At the same time, the people of Boulder have placed a tremendous value on their love of open spaces and mountain parks. There appears to be a successful link between Boulder's ecology and the community of free-spirited entrepreneurs who make this city their center for economic commerce. On the eve of the third millennium, the economy is soaring to all time highs as both public and private enterprises thrive in the presence of this magnificent setting. Yet, it might have been the past and present stewards who have set the tone for Boulder's economic success by limiting development and by preserving the natural setting around Boulder.

In 1955, the "Guide for Growth" was established to develop a comprehensive growth plan by combining the efforts of representatives from the city, the county, and the school board advisory committee. Beginning in 1958, the Blue Line was established, defining a boundary along the foothills above 5,750 feet where building would be prohibited. PLAN-Boulder (People's League for Action Now) was founded in 1959 in "response to an awakening understanding that the attractiveness and individual character of our town are in serious jeopardy." This group called for "a more imaginative and enlightened pattern of community development in the Boulder area." During the early 1960s a fight to save Enchanted Mesa, a 155-acre section of land south and west of Chautauqua Park, came to the forefront. The property owner proposed the construction of a hotel and residential subdivision. Fortunately, the project was never built because the city purchased the land through the efforts of Al Bartlet and PLAN-Boulder. By 1967, PLAN-Boulder had raised citizen awareness to an all-time high, making national headlines by gaining support from Boulder citizens to pass the "Greenbelts for Boulder" sales tax to purchase Open Space lands. Concerned citizens of Boulder had successfully voted for and implemented a progressive plan to assure the quality of life and environment through foresight and participation. By 1990, Boulder was proclaimed one of the most livable cities in America by several of popular monthly publications, including *Outside*, *Walking*, *Bicycling*, *Site Management*, *American Planning* and *MD Magazine*.

In recent years, a vision for the future has been well-thought through with voices heard from stakeholders on all fronts. The Boulder Development Commission stated in a report published in 1991, "Economic development activities are the most cooperative in Boulder's history, with the business community, City and County government, and the University working together very well for the community's future." The Economic Vision Task Force desires a community in 2010 that is "like Boulder today, yet more diverse, continuing to balance our collective concerns for quality of life and the healthy economic base needed to support that quality of life." Boulder's hope for a bright future is possible with continuing participation from concerned citizens and leaders with integrity.

Aerial photo of Boulder and Colorado Rockies

Evening thunderstorm over Boulder—amphitheatre view

"Sustainable business takes responsibility for the effects they have on the natural world."

**—Paul Hawkin,
The Ecology of Commerce**

Easter Lily

Finish work at Unity Church

Morning Lights from Flagstaff Mountain

Deer through my bathroom window

Waiting tables—Walnut Street eatery

"*I dwell in possibility.*"—Emily Dickenson

Sunrise—Chautauqua Park Dining Hall

Saturday Morning—Farmers Market (14th Street)

Summer Evening—Pearl Street Mall

Summer Evening—Pearl and 10th streets

Great Horned Owl

"Where there is no vision, people perish."
—Proverbs 29:18

University Theatre—University of Colorado

View over Libby Hall—University of Colorado

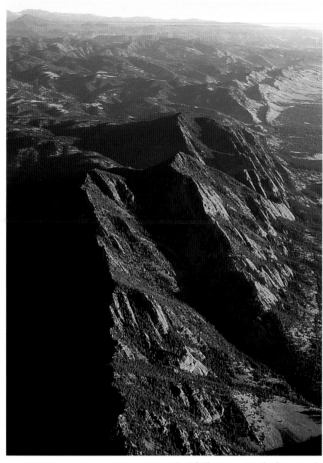

Aerial Flatirons view looking north

Mapleton Hill Home and Flatirons

Old Farm—55th Street

"Whatever you can do, or believe you can, begin it. Boldness has genius, power and magic in it."

—Goethe

Hale Science Buildings' reflection on Varsity Pond'
University of Colorado

Chautauqua Auditorium

Eco-Cycle

A Joint Venture in Recycling and Waste Reduction

Eco-Cycle was created in 1976 by Boulder citizens as a response to growing concern about Boulder's lack of options to increasing amounts of waste in landfills. Over 22 years, Eco-Cycle has emerged as a cooperative partnership between private enterprises, local governments, and Boulder's people. These extensive partnerships have made Eco-Cycle a model organization for many cities and local municipalities throughout the United States.

The organization is guided by people deeply concerned with the live-ability of our city, surrounding areas, and preservation of our natural environment. Dedicated, creative and professional, Eco-Cycle's management and staff have built a recycling facility, and educational program with a core of 900 volunteers on a shoe string budget. Their programs reach everyone of us at our homes, businesses, government offices and schools in an effort to decrease the environmental impacts of our ever-increasing consumer behavior.

Along side Eco-Cycle's production staff, Inmates from our county's jail work each day processing and separating glass, plastic, paper and metal. Currently, 16% or (40,000 tons) of Boulder County's solid waste is recycled annually through Eco-Cycle. Eco-Cycle's mission is to increase the recycled to 50% by 2005 on a path to 75%, and ultimately, 100% percent recovery of formerly wasted resources.

Currently, The Boulder County Recycling and Composting Authority (BCRCA) is considering bids from private, for-profit waste haulers as an alternative to Eco-Cycle's sophisticated, cooperative operational facility and educational organization. BCRCA is evaluating the differences between a for-profit waste hauler versus the cooperative non-profit and volunteer organization of Eco-Cycle. The greatest unmeasurable economic benefit that may be lost if a for-profit hauler takes over the management of the new recycling facilities and programs is the countless volunteer hours and pride our people take in making recycling a part of our community's everyday life. Economically, it appears no for-profit organization could ever match the wide-reaching efficiency, and highly skilled efforts of the current staff, management and volunteers of Eco-Cycle. Hopefully, BCRCA will recognize the importance of Eco-Cycle's community spirit which lies at the heart of the matter as the key to success of future recycling in Boulder.

Inmates prepare for day as forklift operator moves sorted paper

"*Never doubt that a small group of enough thoughtful committed citizens can change the world. Indeed, it is the only thing that ever has.*"

–Margaret Mead

Eco-Cycle employee pushes cans into conveyer

Eco-Cycle employees move plastic

Rainbow over Boulder—view from Flagstaff Mountain

"It takes a long time to become young."

—Pablo Picasso

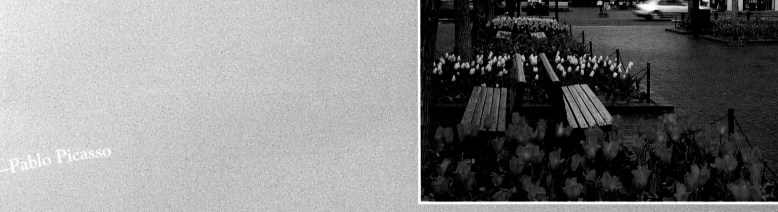

Spring Tulips on Pearl Street Mall

Demolished Building at 28th and Pearl street

Bronze at Pearl and 9th street

Boulder Public Library—Main Branch

"To understand the heart and mind of a person, look not at what he has already achieved, but at what he aspires to."

—*Kahlil Gibran*

Bikes—Williams Village

RTD Bus—Canyon & Broadway

*"The problems we face, and they are nationwide, are new …
demand new and imaginative solutions and immediate action."*
—PLAN–Boulder Newsletter, circa 1959

Sunrise—Pearl East Office Complex

Before Dawn—Valmont Dyke

Chemist in Laboratory

Sunrise—Colorado Highway 36 at Marshall Road

"Now I see the secret of the making
    of the best persons
It is to grow in the open air and to eat and

Boulder Theatre

Clock at Oasis Diner

Sunrise—Road to Brainard Lake

Boulder Skyline—Amphitheatre view

"Only when I have submitted to a place totally, any earth I have shoved around with a bulldozer will be impotent to stir me. The more power I have and use the more likely I am to submit to anything natural and less spiritual power natural things have over me."

—**Wallace Stegner**

Colorado Highway 36 at Superior

Lake Isabelle Drainage–Roosevelt National Forest

OUR GREATER SURROUNDINGS

This is not my native country but
everything in it tells me who I am.

—Wallace Stegner

Our Greater Surroundings

LOOKING FROM THE city center outward, Boulder appears to be defined by its quality of life as much as it is by the open space and mountain parks surrounding it. The natural beauty of Boulder's landscape cannot escape the eye. Walking along Boulder Creek, up a mountain path, or on a trail through Walden Ponds at the break of dawn is a great escape from the day-to-day trappings of urban life. The city's park system and amenities are no less than the natural beauty so easily accessible around us. The surroundings in and near the city open the heart to subtle nuances that can be easily missed on first sight. It takes years to know a place and feel the tempo of its pulse. One visit is never enough, and Boulder is no different.

Yet beyond the inspiring intimacy of Boulder's natural surroundings lie the magnificent, expansive, and diverse landscape of Colorado. Spectacular national and state parks, wilderness areas and recreation areas make Colorado an endless playground for the outdoor enthusiast. The awe-inspiring Rockies cutting through the heart of the state along the Continental Divide is the centerpiece from which all else extends. Rivers flow east and west from here. This is a land so vast it would take a lifetime of exploring to discover its best kept and hidden secrets. This is the adventure waiting for us in Colorado's west.

This territory was roamed by Native Americans over three hundred years ago and "discovered" by early Anglo-European explorers not much more than 150 years ago. Yet today, Colorado still remains a treasure of significant magnitude for the most intrepid and courageous of

modern day adventurers. For those who enjoy the offerings of metropolitan life Denver is just thirty minutes away. Boulder is fortunate to have this expansive landscape at its every turn to move into and enjoy. Beyond Boulder's boundary there is a place it lives within that speaks to the soul of those who find solace connecting with the grand expanse of the natural world all around us.

Cataract Falls—The Gore Range

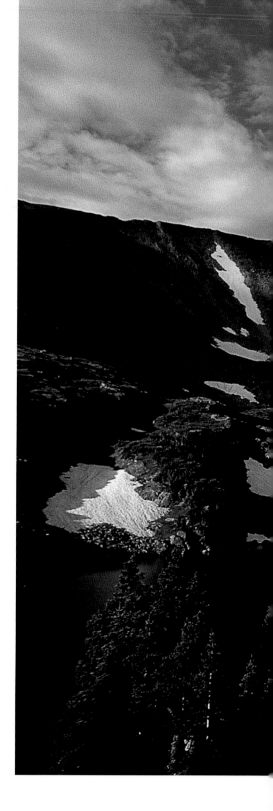

Lake Isabelle—Roosevelt National Forest

Denver Skyline and Mount Evans from the Denver Museum of Natural History

Colorado State Capitol

"Progress is not created by contented people."
—Frank Tyger

Denver Skyline—View City Park

If you don't know where you are,

Trappers Lake—The Flat Tops, White River National Forest

you don't know who you are…

—Wendell Berry

Fence Line & Aspen—Cimmaron River Valley

Dakota Ridge—Settlers Park

"When we pay attention to nature's music, we find that everything on the earth contributes to its harmony."

—Hazrat Inayat Khan

Hanging Lake—Glenwood Canyon

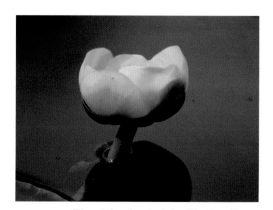

Water Lily—Suprise Lake, The Gore Range

Rippling Brook—Continental Divide, Roosevelt National Forest

Sunrise—Continental Divide
view from Boulder Reservoir

Sunrise—Continental Divide, view from Niwot

"All nature is at the disposal of mankind. We are to work with it. Without it we cannot survive."

—**Hildegard of Bingen**

Mount of the Holy Cross

Longs Peak and Mount Meeker

Sunrise–Drainage to Longs Lake

Fraser River and fire sky at sunrise over the Continental Divide

"Only to the white man was nature a wilderness, and only to him was the land 'infested' with 'wild' animals and 'savage' people. To us it was tame. Earth was bountiful, and we were surrounded with the blessing of the Great Mystery."

—**Chief Luther Standing Bear**
of the Oglala Sioux

Sunrise at North Shore Boulder Reservoir

East Boulder Ranch at White Rocks

"If the world is to be healed through human efforts, I am convinced it will be by ordinary people, people whose love for this life is even greater than their fear. People who can open to the web of life that called us into being, and who can rest in the vitality of that larger body." —Joanna Macy

Fall Reflection on Maroon Lake

Green Mountain Cabin—Boulder Mountain Parks

Sunset—Cat Lake, The Gore Range

Sunrise—The Flatirons, Chautauqua Park

"I reckon I got to light out for the territory.
Aunt Sally's going to adopt me and civilize
me and I can't stand it."

—Mark Twain

Afterwords

Special Thanks

WHEN I STARTED WRITING and selecting photographs for this book, I didn't think there would be more than a few people working with me or helping make this book possible. To nobody's surprise but mine, I have learned just how much support an author/publisher needs in completing a project of this magnitude. To all those friends, acquaintances, and professionals, I offer my most gracious and humble "thank you" for your support, help, and encouragement. These people and organizations include: Josie Heath; Will Toor; Dave Dombrowski; Betty Taylor; Charmayne Bernhardt; Joanne Bolton of Bolton Associates; Sylvia Pettem; Polly Christensen; the librarians at the Carnegie Library; Mo Segal and staff at Celestial Seasonings; David Bolduz and his staff at The Boulder Bookstore; Virginia Patterson at The Printed Page; Ray Toumey at the Chautauqua Association; Sam Abell at *National Geographic*; Peter Kater; Jay Kennis; John and Sally King; Leslie Durgin; and many, many more. I owe one Great Thank you to my family—my Dad for always encouraging me to write and for his love of making home movies; my mom, who passed on in 1982, for always encouraging me to do what I love; and my brother and sister who always said, "follow your dreams." Thank you all.

About the Photographs

I MAKE PHOTOGRAPHS of Boulder and her people because I love this place. For over fourteen years, I have risen before dawn waiting for the sun to rise, and I've chased the last bit of evening light into the dark of night more often than I can remember. Mine is a short career compared to the careers of noted Boulder photographers such as Ed Tangen or Joseph Bevier Sturtevant (alias Rocky Mountain Joe). I have asked a few folks to stop on a hike, to climb a special route or kayak a hole on Boulder Creek at high water; they have more than graciously met my requests, and I thank them for their generosity. I have learned that making a good working photograph is a pursuit that will never end as long as I am capable of picking up a camera. The influences that affect what and how I see are as important as the end results of the photographs themselves. Most importantly, I have learned that the craft and art of photography are a constant adventure. It is the pure sense of innocent pleasure that I get when the photographic conditions are just right that keeps me coming back. Boulder continues to capture my imagination, even as it grows and changes. There is no end to subject matter, but sometimes, sadly, there is a end to the subjects I've seen—both living and landscape—that have now vanished.

Most of the photographs have been made with Nikon 35 mm cameras and lenses, and a few were made with a Pentax 6X7 camera and lenses. The film chosen most often is Fugi Velvia. Composition, exposure, and film speed all vary depending upon the setting, subject, and light. I use a simple technique of researching a subject or location, setting up, composing, exposing, then waiting. I often go to a location or a setting repeatedly until just the right light appears. The best photographs are the one-of-a-kinds that I stumbled upon or created in the thick high action during the most unexpected moment; these are the most precious times. Here, fate and creation collide and are simply inspiration. These are the moments for making the best and happiest photographs which make the fine art of photography a pleasure.

Matters of Deep Concern

B OULDER IS FACING great challenges as it enters the new millennium. The concerns are deep for many reasons. Boulder appears to be losing its character in exchange for economic gain. The issues are more complex than ever. A few issues Boulder is addressing appear due to the increase in people visiting and living in Boulder. Increased traffic, violence and crime, cost of land and housing, and management of public lands (Open Space and Mountain Parks) are a part of the growing population and equally important. The answers are as numerous as the number of people who have a stake in Boulder's well-being. My hope is that a creative minority will rise, leading us to new and imaginative ways to manage, and create change. My greatest concern is a that a polarized citizenry will settle for mediocre solutions. My dream of Boulder is for those of us who truly have this place centered at the heart of our lives and make it our home will come forward to lead us into the next century with a commitment to change for the greatest good, extraordinary vision, purpose and follow through.